This work is dedicated primarily to all the diligent conservationists and volunteers, the unsung heroes who act behind the scenes, doing the field work for the greater good.

About the Authors

James Klucsarits is a volunteer researcher with Hawk Mountain Sanctuary and has been actively studying and banding American Kestrels since 1992. Together with fellow volunteers and interested students, he has been monitoring the long-term reproductive success of kestrels in Eastern Pennsylvania. He also is a professor of biology at Alvernia College and is extremely interested in the conservation of all avian species.

At the time of this writing, Joshua Rusbuldt is a junior at Alvernia College majoring in biochemistry. He began working with Klucsarits during his freshman year and has been an active volunteer in the kestrel conservation effort ever since. With an avid interest in all things science, working with these falcons has helped shift his focus from a textbook idealism to the natural workings of a much larger magnitude.

Authors James R. Klucsarits (left) and Joshua J. Rusbuldt (right)

Key Terms

Asynchronous Hatching – Occurs in birds that begin incubation of eggs prior to laying the last egg of the clutch.

Auricular Feathers – Feathers that cover the opening of a bird's ear.

Barring Pattern – Alternating light and dark feather bands in the plumage of American Kestrels.

Crown Feathers – Feathers that cover the top of the head, specifically behind the eyes.

Primary Feathers – Long or large stiff feathers on the last section of a bird's wing. Primaries are numbered from the innermost to outermost.

Primary Sheaths – Keratinized material that surrounds developing feathers. Sheaths are numbered in the same manner as feathers.

Scapular Feathers – Grouping of feathers on the shoulders and sides of the back.

Sexual Dimorphism – Visual differences in the plumage of the sexes of a species.

Spotting Pattern – Dark circular feather patches adorning the breast and flank of male American Kestrels.

Terminal Band – The culminating band of American Kestrel tail feathers.

Synopsis

The purpose of this work is to illustrate, through digital photography, important anatomical features, and personal observations, the key developmental stages of American Kestrel nestlings from time hatched until fledged. This work will assist anyone working in the field with these falcons, to provide an easy, accurate method of aging young nestlings, and to better plan for nest box visits and banding. This booklet is meant for anyone with an interest in these falcons: from active conservationists, volunteers and students, to avid and amateur bird watchers or anyone displaying a general interest in or appreciation of birds.

THE TIMELINE PROJECT
Photographic Atlas of American Kestrel Nestling Development

22 day old nestlings

(Cover image: 29 day old nestlings)

Contents

THE TIMELINE PROJECT
Photographic Atlas of American Kestrel Nestling Development

Introduction

American Kestrels (*Falco sparverius*) are small, sexually dimorphic falcons sporting a distribution range in our region from Canada to Florida, with a few individuals being year-round inhabitants. After a largely monogamous courtship period ending in late March, female kestrels lay clutches of four to six eggs, with roughly one egg laid per day. Eggs hatch following an incubation period of about twenty-eight days. Once hatched, young nestlings develop to the point of fledging within a period of thirty to thirty-six days (personal observations).

Literature references concerning kestrel development during this month-long period however are scarce. The best guide in circulation that can aid in determining the age and gender of kestrel nestlings is that of Griggs and Steenhof (1993). The primary goal of this project is to clearly illustrate, through colored digital photographs and key measurements and observations, the developmental stages of typical male and female nestlings from time of hatching until fledging. Kestrel developmental variation previously has been correlated with numerous factors including: nestling gender, brood size, asynchronous hatching, parental conditioning (nutrition), and environmental effects (Gard and Bird 1992; Anderson 1993; Weibe and Bortolotti 1995; Dawson and Bortolotti 2000; Massemin et al. 2002). Due to these factors, our focus is to establish ranges of nestling development, which would take into consideration these sources of variation.

As an auxiliary focus, this project hopes to aid field researchers working with the American Kestrels to provide an accurate at-a-glance method of aging young nestlings, and to better plan nest box visits for nestling banding. We hope that such a guide will be significant to those interested in Kestrel conservation, as well as those with a general interest in these falcons.

Methods

Observations were taken on a study area near Hawk Mountain Sanctuary. The study area consists of 1500 square kilometers of open, sparsely wooded fields and farmland in Eastern Pennsylvania. Our site is 30 kilometers north of Reading and 30 kilometers west of Allentown, and includes portions of Berks, Lehigh, and Schuylkill counties. This location has been the site of several kestrel studies in the past (Rohrbaugh and Yahner 1997, Valdez et al. 2000). A conservation program, established by Hawk Mountain, has been maintained by Sanctuary staff and volunteers since 1987 (Rusbuldt et al. 2006). Kestrel broods used in this study nested in established nest boxes mounted to trees and, in a few cases, utility poles.

Our study consisted of measuring and photographing nestlings from primarily three broods during June and early July of summer 2006. These three broods were visited on the day when the first nestling hatched until all of the nestlings fledged from the nest box. This provided us with an accurate starting age from which to base our subsequent measurements. These three broods comprised the entirety of our developmental measurement data, and supplied a total of 14 nestlings for our sample (with brood sizes of 4, 5, and 5 nestlings, respectively). Photographs were taken of other nestlings at different nest box locations, and their estimated ages were then determined using our observed data.

Once the three study broods were identified and photographed at hatching, visits were made during early morning (9am-10:30am) every two days for additional photography. No measurements were taken prior to Day 9 due to a lack of significant primary feather sheaths. For each visit from Day 9 onward, in addition to the digital photographs, we measured with Vernier calipers the length of the fifth primary sheath, and after feather eruption the length of the fifth primary feather. Measurements were always taken from the left wing. Visual qualitative observations (color, feather patterns, gender determination) were noted on the nestlings' appearance each visit. Nestlings were replaced in their nest boxes immediately following measurement sessions, which lasted approximately 15 minutes each.

General Observations

Though our observations have conferred generalized indicators of nestling feather development, it must be stressed that variation is undoubtedly present. Variability factors such as brood size, hatching order, parental provisioning, nestling gender, and environment all readily affect nestling development, thus making a definitive description nigh impossible. The recommended developmental indicators outlined below pool our observations to account for some of this variability.

Distinct observations of feather-sheath development are scarcely noticed until Day 9-10. Prior to this time, nestlings are quite small and completely covered with white down. Nestling size increases during this period, but is difficult to quantify due to the variability factors previously mentioned. Monitoring these nest boxes led us to conclude that aging young during this period is difficult and requires judgment. Accurate aging during this period increases with the observer's experience, as a gestalt is developed.

Once nestlings have reached Day 9-10, key characteristics begin to present themselves. Most notably, feather sheaths begin to appear on the wings and shoulders at this age. Size continues to increase, but the nestlings are still completely down-covered. Patches of colored feathers may appear on the breast at Day 11-12, while the primary sheaths lengthen. Tail feather development is still absent at this stage.

As early as Day 13-14, the primary flight feathers may begin to erupt, though they will be quite small if present. Gender determinations may or may not be able to be made on the basis of primary feather color if they have emerged. At this age tail, flank, and back feathers also begin to erupt. By Day 15-16, gender can be determined with certainty based on typical adult feather coloring and patterning on wings and breast feathers. Back and flank feather density increase as the tail and primaries lengthen.

From Day 17-18 onward, size continually increases as the nestlings become more developed. Gender-specific tail banding as well as breast feather patterning emerges around Day 17-18. The percentage of bodily down steadily decreases as body feathers lengthen and overall feather density increases. Developmental rates of males and females are roughly equal until Day 21-22. During this last week of kestrel development prior to fledging, our observations show that male nestling feather development and size increase slightly more rapidly than females.

8

At-A-Glance Kestrel Development Chart

Nestling Age	Sheath-Primary #5 Length	Characteristic Observations
Day 1-8	Not present	•Small size, increases by day •Sheaths absent, body covered in patchy white down •Difficult to age accurately (Day 4-8)
Day 9-10	Sheaths, if present: 0.6-1.0cm (Mean: 0.82cm)	•Size increases, down covered •Primary sheaths and a few scapular sheaths may be present
Day 11-12	Sheaths: 0.7-1.6cm (Mean: 1.14cm)	•Sheaths developed, distinct •Colored feathers (~10%) appear on breast sides •No tail feathers
Day 13-14	Sheaths: 1.4-2.0cm (Mean: 1.67cm) Primaries, if present: < 0.5cm (Mean: 0.28cm)	•Primaries begin to develop •Tail, flank, & back feathers erupt •Auriculars emerge and darken •Possible to determine sex
Day 15-16	Primaries: 0.2-0.9cm (Mean: 0.48cm)	•Feathers on back/shoulder & flank thicken •Auriculars & primaries lengthen •Sex is determinable
Day 17-18	Primaries: 1.1-2.1cm (Mean: 1.53cm)	•Down prominent on head, lower back, & ~90% of wings •Back & shoulders ~85% feathered •Tail lengthens significantly (White terminal band of males/Dark band of females is visible) •Breast ~50-60% developed (Male spots/Female streaking) •Crown feathers emerge
Day 19-20	Primaries: 2.0-3.2cm (Mean: 2.43cm)	•Entire back almost fully developed ~95% •Upper wings ~20-30% down remaining •Tail lengthens (Females gain 2nd band) •Breast ~80% full •Crown thickens, little down remains on head
Day 21-22	Primaries: 3.3-4.5cm (Mean: 3.71cm)	•Down present ~10-15% upper wings & crown (Females have more than males) •Entire back 100% feathered •Breast ~95% feathered on males (Some down remains on females ~10%)
Day 23-25	Primaries: 5.2-6.2cm (Mean: 5.75cm)	•Tail feathers lengthen (5 bands for females) •Males appear more fully feathered, some bodily down remains on females (lower breast, upper wing, lower back)
> 25 Days	Not measured	•Body size increases as fledging approaches •Resemble miniature adult Kestrels

Recently hatched nestlings

Hatch-Day 8:

From the time of hatching until more than one week's time, nestlings are very small and are completely covered in white, patchy down. Size increases while down density decreases throughout this first week, although primary feather sheaths are completely absent at this stage. Lack of sheaths results in no clear indicator of development, making aging determinations in this range very difficult, especially from the age of Day 4 to 8. Aging in this range relies heavily on personal judgment and experience. When aging nestlings in this range, it is recommended to recheck the box within seven days to more accurately age nestlings.

One day old nestling with egg of sibling

Two day old nestlings

Five day old nestling

Seven day old nestlings

Ten day old nestlings

Day 9-Day 10:

Early into the second week of nestling life, very little developmental indicators are present. Though nestling size increases, they remain fully down covered. At this stage primary and back feather sheaths may be exposed, though small. If sheaths are present[A], they can range from 0.6 to 1.0cm (Mean: 0.82cm).

Eleven day old nestlings

Day 11-Day 12:

During this stage of kestrel development, the prominent indicator of age is the exposure of the primary feather sheaths[B,C], which are very distinct. Sheaths range at this age from 0.7 to 1.6cm (Mean: 1.14cm). Patches of colored feathers begin to emerge on the exterior regions of the breast. Nestlings' backs remain completely down covered and tail feathers are absent.

Eleven day old Male nestling

Twelve day old Female nestling

Fourteen day old Female nestling

Day 13-Day 14:

After two weeks of growth, sheaths are still the dominant anatomical feature with ranges from 1.4 to 2.0cm (Mean: 1.67cm). However, at this stage of development, other indicators of age also begin to emerge. Most notably, primary feathers begin to erupt after approximately two weeks, although at lengths less than 0.5cm (Mean: 0.28cm)[D]. Feathers on the tail[E], flank[F], and back also begin to erupt in this period. The feathers covering the ear opening (auriculars) begin to darken at this age, and constitute another distinctive indicator[G]. Depending on the brood, nestling gender may also be determined at this point by observation of blue-gray coloration on the male wing, and brown and black pigmentation on the female.

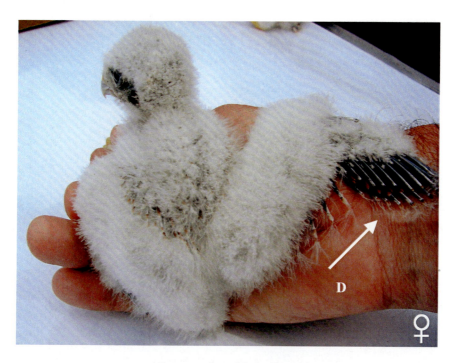

Fourteen day old nestlings

Sixteen day old Female nestling

Day 15-Day 16:

By the age of fifteen or sixteen days, nestling gender can be determined accurately as primary feathers have emerged (Range: 0.2 to 0.9cm, Mean: 0.48cm) and bear the gender-specific pigmentation seen in adult birds (blue-gray coloration of wings on males, brown and black on females)[H]. Exterior flank feathers increase in density, highlighting the spotting patterns of the males and the barring pattern of the females[I]. Back feathers have erupted rather significantly (~30% feathered)[J], and increase in density across much of the dorsal region.

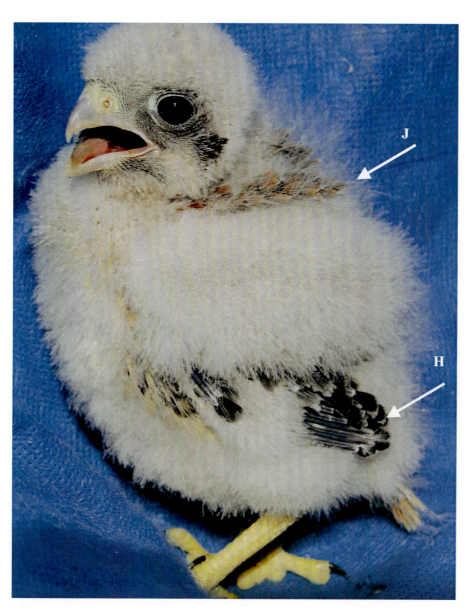

Sixteen day old Male nestling

Eighteen day old Male nestling

Day 17-Day 18:

At this stage, primary feathers continue to lengthen, ranging from 1.1 to 2.1cm (Mean: 1.53cm)[K]. Back feathers have filled in almost completely, with female alternating brown-and-black barring and the male rufous-and-black barring[L]. Flank and breast feathers continue to increase in density as they develop inwards from the exterior[M]. Male breast spotting and female barring increase in intensity. Tail feathers have increased significantly, and terminal banding appears (a white band in males, a dark band in females)[N]. Head remains largely down covered, though crown feathers do begin to emerge[O].

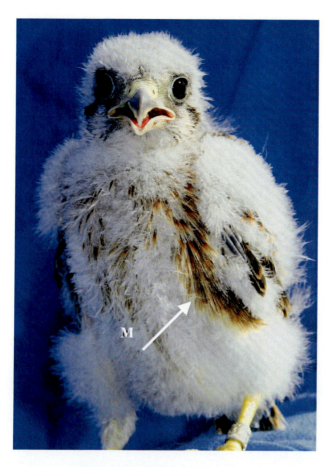

Eighteen day old Female nestlings

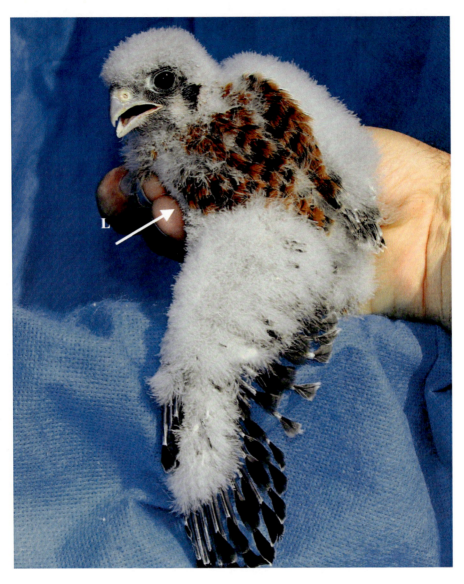

Eighteen day old Male nestling

Twenty day old Female nestling

Day 19-Day 20:

In this time period, primary feathers continue to grow (Range: 2.0 to 3.2cm, Mean: 2.43cm)[P], as do the back[Q] and breast feathers[R], with these areas almost completely feather covered. Tail feathers lengthen, with females showing a second brown band[S]. Crown feather density increases, with little down remaining on the head.

Twenty day old nestlings

Twenty-two day old Female nestling

Day 21-Day 22:

At three weeks of age, primary feathers range in length from 3.3 to 4.5cm (Mean: 3.71cm)[T]. Feathers on the back are almost fully developed (~95-100% feathered)[U], as are breast feathers on males. Female breast feathering, it appears, is at a lower percentage than males. On a whole, more bodily down remains on females than males. Rufous patch on the males' crown is distinctly visible by this age[V]. The tail has lengthened, and male banding pattern (white terminal, black midline, rufous base)[W] is present but no new bands have developed on the female. Head banding pattern of alternating dark and light feathers (mustache, auricular, nape) is highly pronounced[X].

Twenty-two day old nestlings

Twenty-one day old Male nestling

Twenty-three day old nestlings

Day 23-Day 25:

Toward the end of the kestrels' time in their nest boxes, primary feathers reach lengths of 5.2 to 6.2cm (Mean: 5.75cm)[Y]. At this age, kestrels appear as miniature adults. Males appear more fully feathered and have less observable down than females, who still have noticeable patches of down on their lower breast and back, as well as upper wings. Tail feathers lengthen significantly, with females having five alternating bands at this age[Z].

Twenty-five day old nestlings

29

Twenty-five day old nestlings

Twenty-eight day old Male nestling

Post Day 25:

From Day 25, no new measurements or photographs were purposely taken. However, a few candid photographs were taken when we surprised the nestlings still in the boxes. Boxes were monitored over the next week for signs of fledging. During this pre-fledging period, kestrel size increased as nestlings came to fully resemble miniature adults. The fourteen nestlings we observed fledged as early as Day 30 and as late as after Day 32.

Thirty-one day old Female nestlings

Conclusion

Following and photographing the development of these young American Kestrels has been an interesting and rewarding experience. It was a wonderful feeling seeing these birds struggle to exist, to observe their survival through to fledging, and to have the chance to be part of the American Kestrel population in Berks County. We hope we have the opportunity to observe these fledglings on our study site again within the next few breeding seasons. Finally, we hope that you, the reader, enjoyed this reference guide, and join in the support and conservation of wildlife in Pennsylvania and beyond, and that you are encouraged to learn more about the American Kestrel.

Acknowledgments

We offer our thanks to Jim's wife Kelly, for her help and support throughout the project, and especially for her artistic photography, and to Bob and Sue Robertson, our friends and fellow field biologists. We would especially like to thank Keith Bildstein at Hawk Mountain Sanctuary for his editing and technical support. Additional thanks go to Bill Thorne for his help in reviewing our data and Rev. Dr. Richard Rusbuldt for editing. Finally, we send our gratitude to Mark Rittwage at Complete Graphics Inc. for his design advice and layout editing, and to Alvernia College's Dr. Carrie Fitzpatrick for text editing and guidance throughout the publication process and Michele Spotts for photograph editing and cover design.

Twelve day old Female nestling

References

Anderson, David. 1993. Prey size influences female competitive dominance in nestling American Kestrels. *Ecology* **74**: 367-376.

Dawson, R.D. and G.R. Bortolotti. 2000. Reproductive success of American kestrels: The role of prey abundance and weather. *The Condor* **102**: 814-822.

Gard, N.W. and D.M. Bird. 1992. Nestling growth and fledging success in manipulated American Kestrel broods. *Canadian Journal of Zoology* **70**: 2421-2425.

Griggs, G.R. and K. Steenhof. 1993. Photographic guide for aging nestling American Kestrels. U.S. Department of the Interior, Bureau of Land Management, Boise, Idaho.

Massemin, S., E. Korpimäki, V. Pöyri, and T. Zorn. 2002. Influence of hatching order on growth rate and resting metabolism of kestrel nestlings. *Journal of Avian Biology* **33**: 235-244.

Rohrbaugh, R. and R. Yahner. 1997. Effects of macrohabitat and microhabitat on nest-box use and nesting success of American Kestrels. *The Wilson Bulletin* **109**: 410-423.

Rusbuldt, J.J., J.R. Klucsarits, S. Robertson, and B. Robertson. 2006. Reproductive success of American Kestrels using nest boxes in Eastern Pennsylvania, 1992-2005. *Pennsylvania Birds* **20**: 112-117.

Valdez, U., S. Robertson, B. Robertson, and K.L. Bildstein. 2000. Nest box use by American Kestrels (*Falco sparverius*) and European Starlings (*Sturnus vulgaris*) in Eastern Pennsylvania. *Pennsylvania Birds* **14**: 150-153.

Weibe, K. L and G. R. Bortolloti. 1995. Food-dependant benefits of hatching asynchrony in American kestrels *Falco sparverius*. *Behavioral Ecology and Sociobiology.* **36**: 49-57.